LOOS
THROUGH THE AGES

Richard Wood

WAYLAND

Editor: Jason Hook
Book design: Simon Borrough
Series and cover design: Ian Winton

First published in 1997 by Wayland Publishers Ltd, 61 Western Road, Hove, East Sussex, BN3 1JD, England

Find Wayland on the internet at http://www.wayland.co.uk

British Library Cataloguing in Publication Data
Wood, Richard, 1949-
Loos, Through the Ages. - (Rooms Through the Ages)
1. Toilets - History - Juvenile literature 2. Social history
- Juvenile literature
I. Title II. De Saulles, Tony

ISBN 0 7502 2134 8

Printed and bound by G.Canale & CsPA, Turin, Italy

Cover pictures: (Main picture) A seventeenth-century close stool. (Background) An advert for Twyfords toilets in 1905. Title page: A ladies' china chamber pot, made in 1805.

Picture acknowledgements: The publishers would like to thank the following for permission to reproduce their pictures: Ancient Art & Architecture 6(top); Bridgeman Art Library, London 7(left), /Noortman(London)Ltd 8(bottom), /British Library 12(top), 21(top-left), /K&B News Foto, Florence 12(centre), /Museo Correr, Venice 15(bottom), /Singleton Open Air Museum, West Sussex 16(bottom); British Library 13(bottom); CM Dixon 4; Mary Evans *cover*(background), 20(bottom), 27(bottom); Frank Graham/Ron Embleton 8(top); Robert Harding 6(bottom), 14(top); Michael Holford 5, 7(right); Hulton Getty 19(top), 22, 23(bottom), 28(top), 29(top-right); Museum of London 12(bottom); National Portrait Gallery 18(top); National Trust 9, 16(top), 20(top); The Royal Collection © Her Majesty the Queen *cover*(main picture), 18(bottom); Science and Society 1, 19(bottom), 21(bottom), 23(centre), 24, 26, 27(top); Topham 25(bottom); Richard Wood 13(top), 14(bottom), 15(top), 17, 21(top-right), 23(top), 25(top), 28(bottom), 29(top-left, bottom); York Archaeological Trust 10, 11.
All artwork by Tony de Saulles.

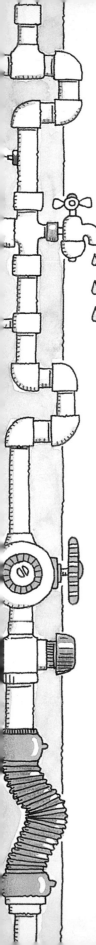

CONTENTS

The Call of Nature

The First Squat

How and where did the first humans 'relieve themselves'? We can only guess that, like other animals, they did not foul their own homes. Probably, they left their caves or shelters and went into the forest. They did not bother to dig permanent toilet pits. They just squatted on the ground, supporting themselves with their hands.

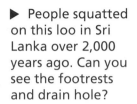

▶ People squatted on this loo in Sri Lanka over 2,000 years ago. Can you see the footrests and drain hole?

A Prickly Problem

What did our ancestors do after going to the toilet? There was no soft toilet paper for prehistoric people. Instead, they selected from a choice of fallen leaves – ranging from broad and floppy, to strong but prickly. In winter, there were always mosses, ferns or stones.

CHAMBER CHAT

Bible Stories
In the Bible, King Eglon was murdered while 'relieving himself in the inner room of the house' (Judges 3: 24). Jehu destroyed Baal's temple, 'and the people have used it for a latrine to this day' (2 Kings 10: 27).

The First Flush

Prehistoric people needed to stay close to rivers for fresh water. But a fast-flowing stream could also carry away waste. A 'squatting place' over the water was an ideal loo, with a built-in flush – though people living further downstream might not be too pleased! Riverside loos have existed since the earliest times.

▲ A loo built about 1450 BC in the king's palace at Knossos, Crete. It was flushed with rainwater carried under the floor in clay pipes.

FANCY THAT!
Sitting Comfortably
Ancient Greek children's potties were shaped like armchairs, complete with armrests and a back. This Greek vase (below) is decorated with a picture of a child on a potty, playing with a rattle. The water jug on the floor was for cleaning out the potty after use.

WC, BC.

Archaeologists have found the world's oldest water closets, or 'WCs', at Mohenjo-Daro in north-west India. In 2000 BC, this great city had about 40,000 inhabitants. Many homes had their own private loos. Pots of water were tipped into the loos to flush the contents through pipes, into drains which ran under the streets outside.

◄ A 2,500-year-old Greek vase, showing a child sitting on a luxury potty.

The Cloaca Room

Clean if not Decent

The Romans, who ruled Britain from AD 43 to AD 410, were famous for their clever technology. Most Roman homes had proper drains to carry their waste away. For the Roman citizen, going to the loo was a social event to be shared. They would have thought us very odd going into a little room and locking the door behind us.

Roman cities had many public conveniences. In AD 315, there were 144 public loos in Rome alone, a greater number per person than in most towns today. Some Roman loos were very large. The Romans went there to meet their friends, to exchange news and gossip.

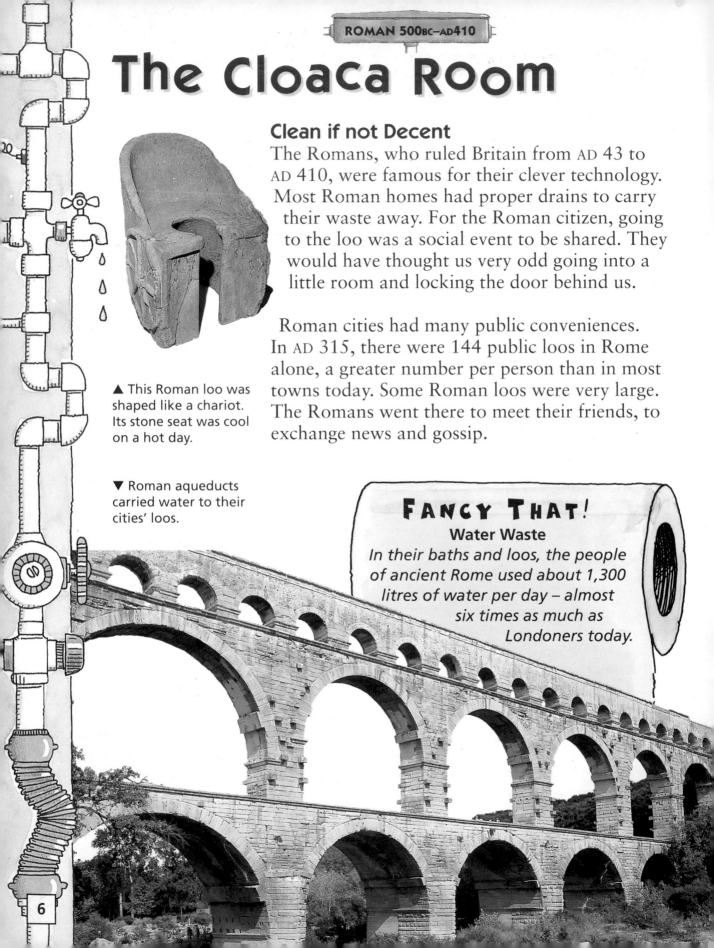

▲ This Roman loo was shaped like a chariot. Its stone seat was cool on a hot day.

▼ Roman aqueducts carried water to their cities' loos.

FANCY THAT!
Water Waste
In their baths and loos, the people of ancient Rome used about 1,300 litres of water per day – almost six times as much as Londoners today.

▼ A Roman dolphin mosaic, in Utica, North Africa, from about AD 250.

▲ These public loos at 'Hadrian's Baths' in Libya could seat about fifty people. They were once decorated with mosaic floors and fountains.

The dolphin was a favourite decoration in Roman public lavatories. At Timgad, in North Africa, a carved dolphin armrest separated each seat.

Lavatory Gods

The Romans took cleanliness so seriously that they even had gods to guard their toilets. Stercutius was god of dirt, and Crepitus god of the loo. The 'goddess of the common sewer' was called Cloacina. Public lavatories, called *cloaca* in her honour, had shrines where people made offerings to Cloacina. Rome's sewers were called the Cloaca Maxima. They were designed by a man named Tarquenius Superbus, and date back to 400 BC.

Do you have pictures on your loo walls? It is said that Diana, Princess of Wales, decorated her loo at Kensington Palace with cartoons of her ex-husband. The walls and floors of Roman loos were often painted with gods and goddesses. Some had notices telling users to keep them clean – or else!

CHAMBER CHAT

Messy Nessy
Many nicknames for the loo come from the Romans. 'Privy' comes from the Latin *privatus* (private); 'latrine' from *latrina*, the name for the soldiers' toilets; and 'nessy' (short for 'necessary') from the Latin *necessarium*.

Roman Remains

A Sticky Situation

Have you ever sat on the loo, then realized, too late, that the paper has run out? The Romans never had this problem. Instead of paper, they used a piece of natural sponge fixed on a short wooden handle. In front of the loo was a water channel where people dipped their sponge-sticks. The same sponges were shared by everyone who used the loo.

▼ Soldiers using the latrines at Housesteads, a fort on Hadrian's Wall in Northumberland. Notice the sponge and washing facilities.

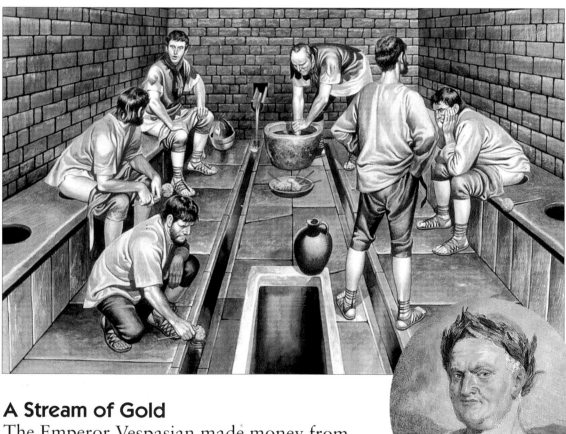

A Stream of Gold

The Emperor Vespasian made money from public urinals that he built in the amphitheatre called the Colosseum. People had to pay to use them. Their urine was then collected and sold to cloth-makers, who used it to remove grease from wool.

▲ Vespasian, who invented the pay toilet.

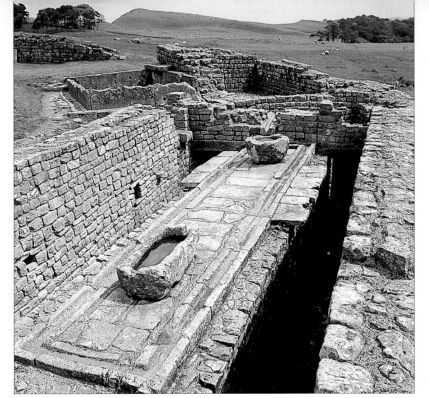

◀ The remains of the latrines at Housesteads. They were built in AD 122. Men sat close together, eight on each side. Water was collected in tanks, and used to flush out the channels under the seats.

A Soft Touch

Before going about his business, a Roman soldier would first select his sponge-stick. He would then clean this in the salty water or vinegar that was provided. Most Roman loos were designed with the sponge-stick in mind. The keyhole-shaped hole in the loo allowed the user to poke the sponge in and wipe himself. Rich Roman ladies did not like to use the sponge. They preferred the soft touch of an ostrich feather.

Home Comforts

Many poor Romans lived in apartment blocks called *insulae*. Here, many families had to share the same loo. To help with drainage, insulae were often built directly over rivers, or sewers such as the Cloaca Maxima. The homes of rich Romans had their own private loos. These were built near the front door, and emptied into the sewers running beneath the pavement outside.

FANCY THAT!
A Wee Cure
Roman dyers and weavers washed their cloth in urine. The writer Pliny noticed that they never suffered from gout. Older people today remember bathing their legs in warm urine as a cure for chilblains.

CHAMBER CHAT
A Snap of the Fingers
With a click of the fingers (*concrepare digitos*), rich Romans could summon a slave to bring a special cloak and potty, for on the spot relief.

Back to Pits and Pots

Saxon Cesspits

The Romans left Britain in AD 410. The Saxons who succeeded them had little time for Roman luxury loos. They preferred to use pots, or squat over deep cesspits outside their homes. These were easy to dig, and their contents could be used to manure the land. Some people used loos like this as recently as the 1950s.

▼ Remains in Viking cesspits, like the lump shown here, can tell us what the Vikings ate, and what diseases they suffered from.

▲ Archaeologists found the original loo seat preserved in this 800-year-old cesspit.

Viking Visits

In the ninth century, fierce Viking raiders conquered many parts of Britain. Traces of the deep cesspits that they dug have been uncovered at Jorvik, the Viking city at York.

FANCY THAT!

Holy Odours
Some Saxon churchmen disagreed with the old saying, 'Cleanliness is next to godliness'. They said that being dirty was good, as it reminded people of how sinful they were.

Digging for Worms

From digging up and studying the contents of their loos, we know that many Viking people suffered very badly from worms – not just tiny ones but fat, wriggly creatures several centimetres long. Some Vikings also ate hard seeds from blackthorn bushes. These were probably to help them go to the loo when they were constipated.

Chamber Chat

Murder Most Foul

In 1016, the Saxon king, Edmund Ironside, was murdered while using the loo. A chronicle records that he was 'struck with a spear in the fundament while at the withdraught to purge nature'.

Some historians believe that the Vikings drank each other's urine. If they had first eaten a certain sort of mushroom, this made them strong and fearless.

▼ This Viking enjoys a quiet moment in the reconstructed loo at York.

The Midden Ages

Medieval Muck

Our medieval ancestors were not the cleanest of people. In the countryside, they placed smelly heaps of excrement, called 'middens', far too close to houses. In cities, they thought nothing of wading through human and animal filth on the streets. In many places, dirt and sewage were just left to pile up. In 1281, it took a gang of men a week to clear twenty tonnes of filth from the pit outside London's Newgate prison.

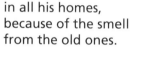

▲ King Henry III, who in 1245 built new loos in all his homes, because of the smell from the old ones.

▶ An open-air medieval loo in Sicily.

'Gardez l'eau!'

Potties called 'pysse pottes' were kept in most medieval homes. Streets had open drains, so it was easy to empty the pots. You just tipped the contents out of the window. The usual warning cry was 'Gardez l'eau', French for 'watch the water'. The word 'loo' probably comes from 'l'eau'.

▲ This medieval pysse pot could be carried without splashing.

▲ A Cambridge street known as 'Piss Pot Lane'. You can guess what students did out of their windows.

Hold your Nosegay

In 1358, there were only four public loos, known as 'common privies', in the whole of London. The largest of these, on London Bridge, emptied straight into the River Thames. In many towns, drains ran directly into the same rivers that supplied drinking water. No wonder rich people sniffed at bunches of sweet-scented flowers, called 'nosegays', to avoid breathing in the stench of their surroundings.

Medieval people sometimes went outside to perch over a cesspit, rather than use a potty. A law of 1189 said that cesspits must be at least two feet (0.8 metres) away from the neighbours' walls. Unfortunately, the law was not always obeyed. In 1328, a man named William Sprot complained that his neighbours had filled their cesspit until it was overflowing, and the filth was seeping through the wall into his house.

▲ A medieval doctor examines a jar of urine. Some people used their own urine as an early-morning mouthwash.

A Convenient Cloister

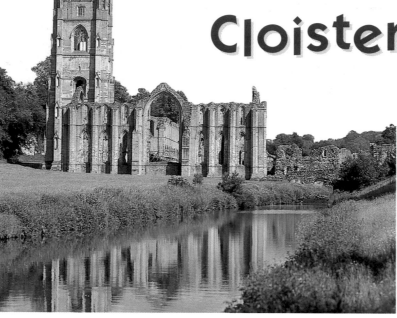

◄ At Fountains Abbey, Yorkshire, the monks' loos emptied directly into the river.

▼ Medieval loos at Langley Castle, in Northumberland, were in arched cubicles so their users had some privacy.

Canterbury Tales

Both medieval castles and monasteries were built beside, or even over, rivers for drainage. A 'Good Loo Guide' would have given the top prizes to the monasteries. When the Black Death killed almost half the population of Britain in 1349, not one monk in Canterbury died, thanks to their clean living conditions and toilet facilities.

Monasteries were protected from the filth of the medieval streets. Their loos were sited in the 'reredorter'. This special toilet block stood at the end, or 'rear', of the dormitory, or 'dorter', above a water-flushed drain.

CHAMBER CHAT

Ancient Rites
In Durham Monastery, 'The Privies [were] closed on either side so that they could not see one another when they were in that place.'

In the Garderobe

Foul-smelling outdoor pits were not popular with rich people in medieval times. Instead, they had little rooms built jutting out from the walls of their chambers. Ideally, these were over a moat, but if this was not possible, a fenced-off pit would do. In castles, these little rooms were known as 'garderobes'.

▲ Garderobe chutes at Norwich Castle.

Garderobe was a polite name for the loo. It really means the same as 'wardrobe', which is also a form of private closet. Medieval castles were so strongly built that the shafts for the garderobes were built into the thickness of their stone walls.

Chamber of Horrors

Castle cesspits could be dangerous places. In 1184, Emperor Frederick Barbarossa of Germany met with his nobles at Erfurt Castle. So many of them followed him when he went into the garderobe to use the loo that the floor gave way. The Emperor grabbed the iron window bars and saved himself, but many others fell to an unpleasant death. When King Edward II of England lost the crown in 1327, he is said to have been tortured in the stinking garderobe pit of Berkeley Castle.

▶ Emperor Barbarossa (1123–1190), who nearly came to a sticky end. Almost every act of a medieval king was public, even using the loo.

Kings and Jakes

◄This closet at Knole, a house in Kent, contains the potty used by King Charles II, who ruled from 1660 to 1685.

CHAMBER CHAT

Spending a Penny
'No man must make water within the courts upon pain of one penny,' said a 1566 set of rules for servants.

The Great House of Easement

Compared to medieval arrangements, Tudor loos were not to be sniffed at. Henry VIII's courtiers at Hampton Court shared a 'great house of easement', with twenty-eight seats on two different levels. It emptied into brick-lined drains which carried the waste under the palace moat and into the River Thames. The royal loos were cleaned by Phillip Long and his team of 'gong scourers'. These were boys small enough to crawl along the drains.

Tudor people would happily 'pluck a rose' (urinate) anywhere – in chimneys, corners of rooms or the street. In Edinburgh, you could hire a portable toilet – a bucket and a tent-like cloak – from men who wandered the streets crying, 'Wha wants me for a bawbee?'

▼ This simple loo jutted out from a Tudor farmhouse bedroom.

P for Pepys

Samuel Pepys, in his famous diary, recalls when his wife was 'taken short' during a play. He 'was forced to go out of the house with her ... and there in a corner she did her business'. At St Paul's School in London, the boys' urine was collected in tubs and sold to tanners and dyers. The profits went to school funds.

> ## FANCY THAT!
> ### Dirty Habits
> *Remains from cesspits show that medieval and Tudor people used a variety of things to wipe themselves. The poor still used leaves, moss or stones. Better-off people cut up their worn-out clothes into handy-sized pieces. Even monks' old habits ended up as neat little squares hanging in the rere-dorter.*

'The jakes' was the expression for the loo used by almost everyone in Tudor times, even Shakespeare. In many small country houses, the jakes stuck out from the wall and emptied into a pit below. Ashes were thrown on the pit to reduce the smell. In some houses, like the one on the right, the jakes emptied directly into a river.

▼ Rivers still made the best drains. Can you see the loo jutting out from the wall?

The Lap of Luxury

Royal Stools

While his servants shared the house of easement, the king did his royal business on a luxurious 'close stool'. This was a large, lidded box containing a bucket and water tank, with a padded seat. Henry VIII's close stool had a velvet seat, trimmed with silk ribbons and studded with gold nails. Not to be outdone, in 1538 Scotland's King James V spent £58 on green damask cloth to decorate 'a pavilion for his stool of ease'.

▲ Henry VIII, whose sturdy close stool accompanied him on journeys.

A Groom with a View

Royal 'stool rooms' were supervised by the 'Groom of the Stool'. It was his job 'to give attendance upon the King's highness when he goeth to make water in his bedchamber'. Regulations said that he should have with him 'linen to wipe the nether end ... a basin and ewer, and on his shoulder a towel'. These royal arrangements were not changed until Queen Victoria installed the first water closets 300 years later.

◀ A luxurious seventeenth-century close stool from Hampton Court.

Royal Flush

With a swoosh of water, a new era in the history of the loo began in 1596. In this year, Sir John Harington invented the first water closet with a proper flush. Harington built his WC in his house at Kelston, Somerset. It was used by Elizabeth I, who was so impressed that she had one built at Richmond Palace.

CHAMBER CHAT

Harington's Moral
Harington wrote: 'To keep your houses sweet, cleanse privy vaults: to keep your souls as sweet, mend privy fault.'

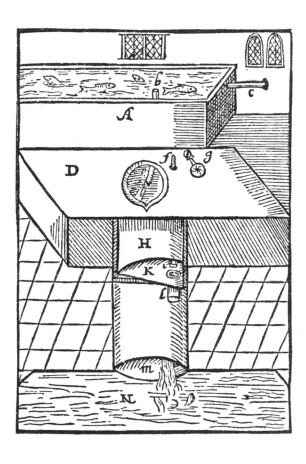

◀Harington's diagram shows how to work his WC. Fill the bowl (H) by moving the lever (g). Pull the handle (f) to empty into the drain (m).

Ajax

Harington wrote a humorous book about the morals of using loos called *The Metamorphosis of Ajax*. 'Ajax' is a joke – he means 'a jakes'. Unfortunately, Harington's WC was knocked down after his death and his idea was forgotten. It was almost 200 years before the WC was re-invented.

▼ In this drawing from *The Metamorphosis of Ajax*, the Devil taunts a priest for praying while sitting on a draught.

FANCY THAT!
The Queen's Pleasure
Queen Elizabeth I was a clean queen. She took a bath every year, 'whether she needed it or not'. King Charles I was a more messy monarch. After he stayed in Oxford, his hosts were disgusted by the filthy state of his rooms.

What a Potty

Hidden Treasures

Where would you keep a potty? In the 1700s, the most likely place was in the dining room. Sideboards and chests of drawers had special potty holders. Some were even fitted with a built-in seat. Just pull out a drawer, or lift a lid, and you could use it where it was. Then, shut it away for a servant to empty later. Any piece of furniture that contained a potty became known as a 'commode'.

▲ A commode hidden in the dining room at Penrhyn Castle, Wales.

FANCY THAT!
Potty Politics
Lord Hervey was an absent-minded government minister. Once, at a dinner, he urgently needed a potty and went behind a window curtain to use it. When he reappeared at the table, he had forgotten to put his trousers back on. This 'caused much amusement to the ladies'.

▶ Louis XIV, who ruled France from 1643 to 1715, had his potty fitted into a comfortable chair. The man behind was the 'official wiper'.

Down the Pan

Most loos were far too smelly to have indoors. Around 1750, a new type called the 'pan closet' was invented. At the bottom of the closet was a pan of water designed to seal in unpleasant odours. It was not very effective, as it was impossible to keep this pan clean. One angry plumber described the pan closet as 'a filthy and corrupt apparatus'.

▲ At the pull of a lever, the pan closet's contents were tipped down the drain.

▲ An 1805 cartoon, showing a man on the pan.

Sweet Smell of Success

At last, in 1775, a watchmaker called Alexander Cummings invented the first modern water closet. A sliding valve kept water in a basin, then flushed waste through a smell-proof tank at the pull of a lever. Only occasionally did the valve get stuck!

▼ The painted face in this Georgian 'frog potty' is saying: 'Oh dear me, what do I see?'

CHAMBER CHAT
Potty Poems
This verse was written inside Georgian potties:
'Keep me clean and use me well,
And what I see I will not tell.'

In 1778, Joseph Bramah replaced the valve with a hinged flap. It was so reliable that people believed potties would become a thing of the past. 'The Piss Pot's Lament' was a popular poem about a potty nobody wanted to use.

A Great Stink

A Long Queue

During the nineteenth century, the population of Britain increased rapidly. Unfortunately, the number of loos did not. In the overcrowded slums of cities like Edinburgh, Manchester and London, many poor families had to share a single loo. Sewers, if there were any, emptied straight into rivers, like London's filthy Thames.

Movements for Reform

Sir Edwin Chadwick's report of 1842, *Sanitary Conditions of the Labouring Classes*, blamed bad loos for the regular outbreaks of typhus and cholera. Chadwick suggested replacing leaky brick drains with pottery pipes, and said that for only four pounds, a house could be fitted with its own sink, drain and WC.

FANCY THAT!
Plump Plums
Country people emptied their cesspits using a long-handled 'shittus scoop', and recycled the contents in their gardens. Potatoes and plums grew especially well on human manure.

▼ A cartoon from 1855. It shows the Victorian scientist Michael Faraday asking Father Thames to clean himself up.

CHAMBER CHAT

State Papers
On seeing pieces of toilet paper floating in the River Cam, Queen Victoria asked what they were. 'Those, ma'am,' her host replied, 'are notices warning people not to bathe.'

A Stink in the House

After another cholera epidemic, the Government took notice. The Public Health Act of 1848 said every new house should have a water closet or ash-pit privy. Improvements were slow. By 1860, most London homes had a fresh water supply for a few hours each day. But very few were connected to sewers of any sort. In 1858, 'The Great Stink' from the polluted River Thames caused Parliament to close down.

◄A Victorian commode. The pot was taken out and emptied into a cesspit.

▼ Night soil men with their barrel. They worked at night because of the stink and flies.

▲ This commode was used by Queen Victoria when travelling in her own railway carriage.

Dirty Work

Most town dwellers relied on 'night soil men' to empty their cesspits, in much the same way as the medieval 'gongfermors' had done centuries earlier. For a long time, the council in Manchester refused to install proper WCs because of the cost of building water pipes and sewers. In 1878, Liverpool became one of the first cities to have a constant water supply, something that most Londoners did not get until the 1890s.

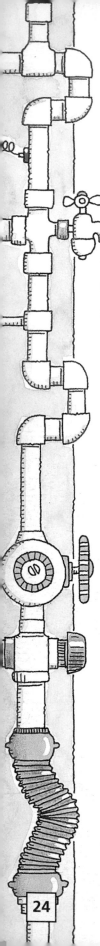

Sanitary Reform

Prince of Plumbing

'If I were not a prince, I'd be a plumber,' said the Prince of Wales, Queen Victoria's eldest son. He had reason to know the importance of good plumbing. He once nearly died of cholera, caught from bad drains at a Yorkshire country house. The prince supported the 'Sanitary Reform Movement', which after 1850 campaigned for better hygiene. Not everyone was impressed. 'Sanitary Reform is bunk [nonsense],' complained one Member of Parliament.

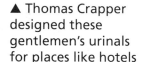

▲ Thomas Crapper designed these gentlemen's urinals for places like hotels and stations.

Pipe Dreams

Flushing loos seemed more hygienic than cesspits. They were pleasant to use, easier to keep clean and less trouble to empty. But they only worked if houses had piped water and sewage pipes. Many homes did not have these things until the twentieth century.

Installing efficient loos in houses was one thing, but what about public conveniences? Victorian inventors like Thomas Crapper designed loos suitable for every location, from elaborate hotel urinals, like those shown above, to simple trough loos for use in schools.

Chamber Chat

Thrifty Dodges
A servant wrote to Queen Victoria to describe the Prince of Wales' savings at Windsor Castle: 'We all admire the various little economical thrifty dodges here. In the WCs – NEWSPAPER SQUARES!'

Earth to Earth

Imagine a loo that flushed earth, not water. This is how the 'Earth Closet' worked. It was invented in 1860 by the Reverend Samuel Moule as a loo for places without piped water. Moule's loo used a bucket, with a tank at the back containing dry earth or crushed cinders. When you pulled the lever, a measured amount of earth dropped into the bucket to cover the latest offering.

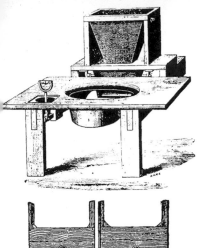

▲ Moule's Earth Closet. The friendly two-seater version was designed for use in schools.

▼ A Victorian toilet bowl, with early examples of toilet roll.

Curl Papers

The first loo paper, 'Gayety's Medicated Paper', appeared in 1857. It was called 'curl papers', and came in flat packs. Chemists sold it from under the counter, because people were embarrassed to see it displayed. Toilet rolls were first sold in 1928. Soft paper was introduced in 1932, but was unpopular at first! In 1957, coloured paper brightened up loos for the first time.

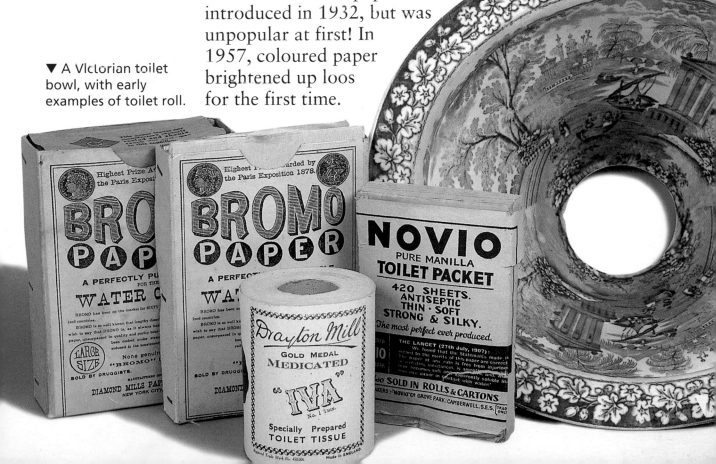

The Race for Perfection

Flushed with Success

From the 1850s, the race was on to design the perfect loo. New models were tested at sanitary competitions to see which had the most powerful flush. At the 1884 Health Exhibition, one WC used two gallons of water to flush ten apples, one sponge, four pieces of paper, three inflatable objects and some grease smeared round the sides.

FANCY THAT!
The Bare Facts
The first time many Victorian ladies used a flushing loo was at the Great Exhibition of 1851. Curious to see how it worked, they peered below, only to see a reflection of their own behinds. Not everyone liked what they saw, which explains why patterned loo bowls became so popular.

Stinking Rich

In the field of loos, the British led the world. Even the Americans imported most of their loos from Britain. Stephen Hellyer's luxury 'Optimus' model was supplied to the Queen and the Houses of Parliament, and exported to India, China and Australia. His simple 'Jar' model was made 'for rough, even violent, treatment as in prisons, police courts, asylums and schools'.

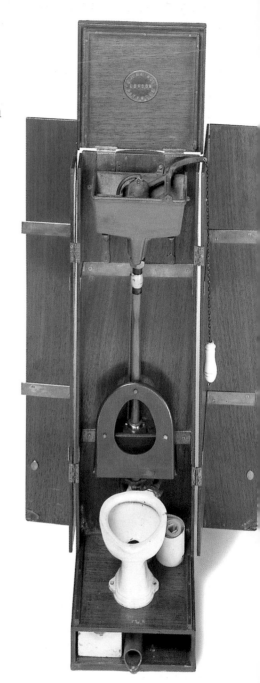

▲ George Jennings made this working model to demonstrate a new water closet to his customers.

Crapper's Creation

Every time an early Victorian loo was flushed, gallons of water were wasted. But if you look in the cistern of a modern loo, you will see a bell-shaped device. This allows only a certain amount of water up the pipe. This 'Water Waste Preventer' was developed in the 1880s by Thomas Crapper.

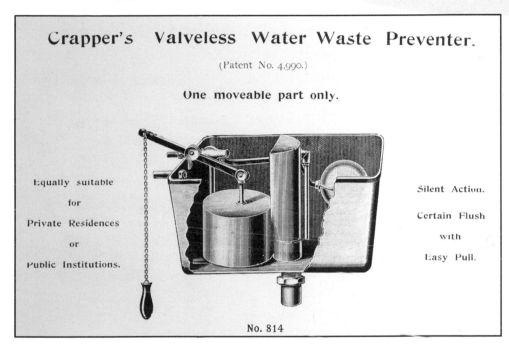

Crapper's Valveless Water Waste Preventer.

(Patent No. 4,990.)

One moveable part only.

Equally suitable for Private Residences or Public Institutions.

Silent Action.
Certain Flush with Easy Pull.

No. 814

◄The design for Crapper's Water Waste Preventer. Crapper's loos were installed in Buckingham Palace.

The Year of the Loo

Two great improvements in loo design were made in 1885. One was the new, improved 'syphonic system' to help clear waste, which we still use. The other was Joseph Twyford's 'Unitas' model. This was the first 'pedestal' loo, which stood on its own without a supporting wooden case. At first, people disliked its appearance. But when doctors recommended it as more hygienic, the idea caught on. Soon, people would sit on nothing else.

◄An advert from 1905, for Twyfords' latest loo.

Clean and Decent

▲ The outside loo of a Liverpool slum, in 1959.

Bucket and Chuck it

After all those amazing Victorian inventions, you might expect everyone in the twentieth century to have a well-equipped bathroom. In fact, many people in rural areas still used privies at the bottom of the garden until the 1960s. In parts of Norfolk, the night soil men did their rounds until 1989. Some country people still have to bury toilet waste in their gardens – a system known as 'bucket and chuck it'.

Euro-Loos

How does your loo work? British law says WCs must use syphons, like those invented in the 1880s. But most European loos now use valves instead. Some people say they give a more powerful flush. The introduction of European law may see 'Euro-loos' invading British bathrooms.

▼ A modern coin-operated public loo. Some people have a fear of being locked in!

FANCY THAT!
Bolting Bacteria
Flushing the loo pollutes the air! When you flush the loo, germs or 'bacteria' are forced into the air, particularly if you flush with the lid down. In 1966, the medical journal The Lancet *said that flushing 'produces a bacterial aerosol'.*

A News Flush

The loo of the future will probably be the 'Vacuum Water Closet', or VWC. When flushing, the lid is closed to form an air-tight seal. At the push of a button, an electric motor creates a vacuum and all the water and waste are sucked out with a loud slurping sound. You might have seen a loo like this on a ship or an aeroplane.

The Honey Cart

In the 1950s, Wally Feeke emptied loos in Litcham, Norfolk, into his horse-drawn 'honey cart'. One hot day, Wally hung his jacket on the cart. The horse shied, and the jacket slid into the full tank. Rolling up his sleeves, Wally fished it out. 'That jacket won't be much cop now,' called a friend. 'It's not me jacket I'm after,' replied Wally, 'It's the sandwiches wot's in me pocket!'

▲ A VWC on a ferry. A notice says: 'Do not put anything in the toilet unless you have eaten it first.'

▼ Emptying a loo bucket into the 'honey cart', in about 1950.

▲ The world's tallest toilet is housed in an old chimney.

CHAMBER CHAT
Comic Relief
Today, people see the funny side of loos. A well-known book called *The Specialist* is all about Lem Putt, a carpenter who builds outdoor privies.

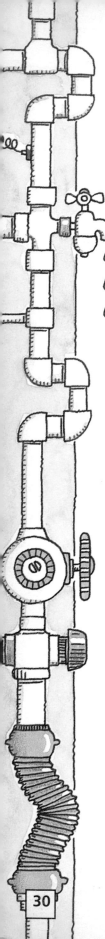

CHAIN OF EVENTS

2000 BC	Flush loos are in use at Mohenjo-Daro, India.
1450 BC	Palace loos are in use at Knossos, Crete.
AD 75	Emperor Vespasian has public loos built in Rome.
AD 122	Soldiers' loos are built at Housesteads fort, on Hadrian's Wall.
AD 1016	The Anglo-Saxon king Edmund Ironside is murdered on the loo.
AD 1184	Emperor Frederick of Germany falls in his cesspit.
AD 1189	A law orders cesspits to be built away from houses.
AD 1245	King Henry III has new loos built in all his homes.
AD 1327	King Edward II is tortured in a garderobe.
AD 1530	The 'Great House of Easement' is built at Hampton Court.
AD 1596	Sir John Harington invents the flushing water closet.
AD 1750	Pan closets are fitted in some large houses.
AD 1775	Alexander Cummings invents the modern WC.
AD 1778	Joseph Bramah invents a reliable WC, using a hinged flap to flush water.
AD 1842	Edwin Chadwick publishes *Sanitary Conditions of the Working Classes*.
AD 1842	The first WC is installed in Buckingham Palace.
AD 1848	The First Public Health Act says all new homes should have loos.
AD 1857	The first toilet paper is sold in Britain.
AD 1860	Samuel Moule invents the Earth Closet.
AD 1861	Crapper & Co start business in Chelsea.
AD 1885	Joseph Twyford invents the 'Unitas' pedestal loo.
AD 1900	90% of London homes now have piped water.
AD 1928	Toilet paper is first sold in rolls.
AD 1959	The Vacuum WC is invented in Sweden.
AD 1996	A wedding is held in a public lavatory for the first time, in Taiwan.
AD 1997	Europe presses Britain to install valve WCs.

PLACES TO PAY A VISIT

Alternative Technology Centre, Machynlleth, Gwynedd, Wales. Tel: 01654 702400
Shows modern alternative loos, from home-made 'pee cans' to self-composting loos.

Fountains Abbey, Nr. Ripon, Yorkshire. Tel: 01765 609999
Ruined remains of monks' loos and water pipes.

Housesteads Roman Fort, Nr. Haltwhistle, Northumberland. Tel: 01434 344363
Includes the ruins of a Hadrian's Wall toilet block.

North of England Open Air Museum, Beamish, Durham. Tel: 01207 231811
The loos of rich and poor from the early 1900s.

Science Museum, London. Tel: 0171 938 8000
Shows the development of the WC, with examples you can flush.

Weald and Downland Museum, Singleton, W. Sussex. Tel: 01243 811348
Has a reconstructed loo of about 1450.

GLOSSARY

Bawbee	A coin worth three Scottish pennies
Cesspit	A deep pit for burying human waste
Cistern	A water tank
Close stool	A box enclosing a potty
Closet	A small, private room, or cupboard
Commode	A piece of furniture designed to hold a potty
Cubicle	A small private room
Fundament	The bottom
Garderobe	A loo in a medieval castle
Gongfermor	Someone who emptied medieval cesspits
Latrine	A public loo
Metamorphosis	A complete change or transformation
Midden	A dirt heap
Mosaic	A pattern made with coloured stones
Nessy	A northern word for the loo
Nether end	The bottom
Nosegay	A bunch of sweet-smelling flowers
Pavilion	A portable building or tent
Pedestal	A pillar or support
Penance	An action to make up for bad deeds
Privy	A loo, from the Latin for 'private'
Purge	To clean out
Rere-dorter	Site of the loos in a monastery
Scourers	Cleaners of drains and sewers
Thrifty	Economical, money-saving
Urinals	Gents' stand-up loos, for urine only
Water closet	A loo with a flush
Withdraught	A word for the loo, from 'withdraw'

BOOKS TO READ

Harris, M. *Cotswold Privies* (Countryside Books, 1995)
Kerr, D. *Keeping Clean* (Watts Books, 1995)
Kilroy, R. *The Compleat Loo* (Victor Gollancz, 1984)
Lambton, L. *Temples of Convenience* (Gordon Fraser, 1987)
Palmer, R. *The Water Closet* (David & Charles, 1989)
Reyburn, W. *Flushed with Pride* (Pavilion Books, 1989)
Turner, J. *East Anglian Privies* (Countryside Books, 1996)

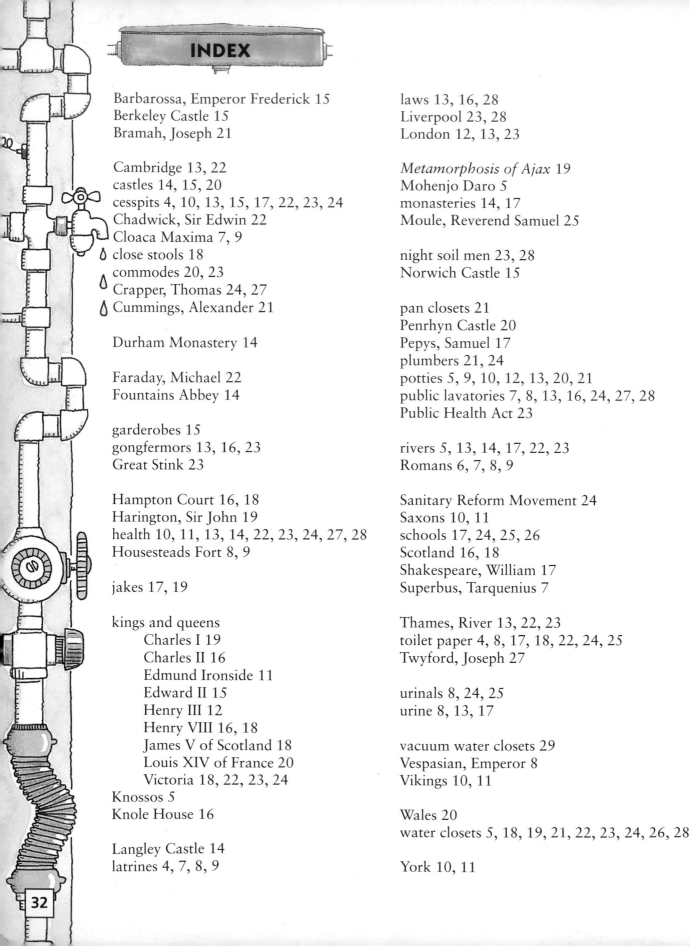

INDEX